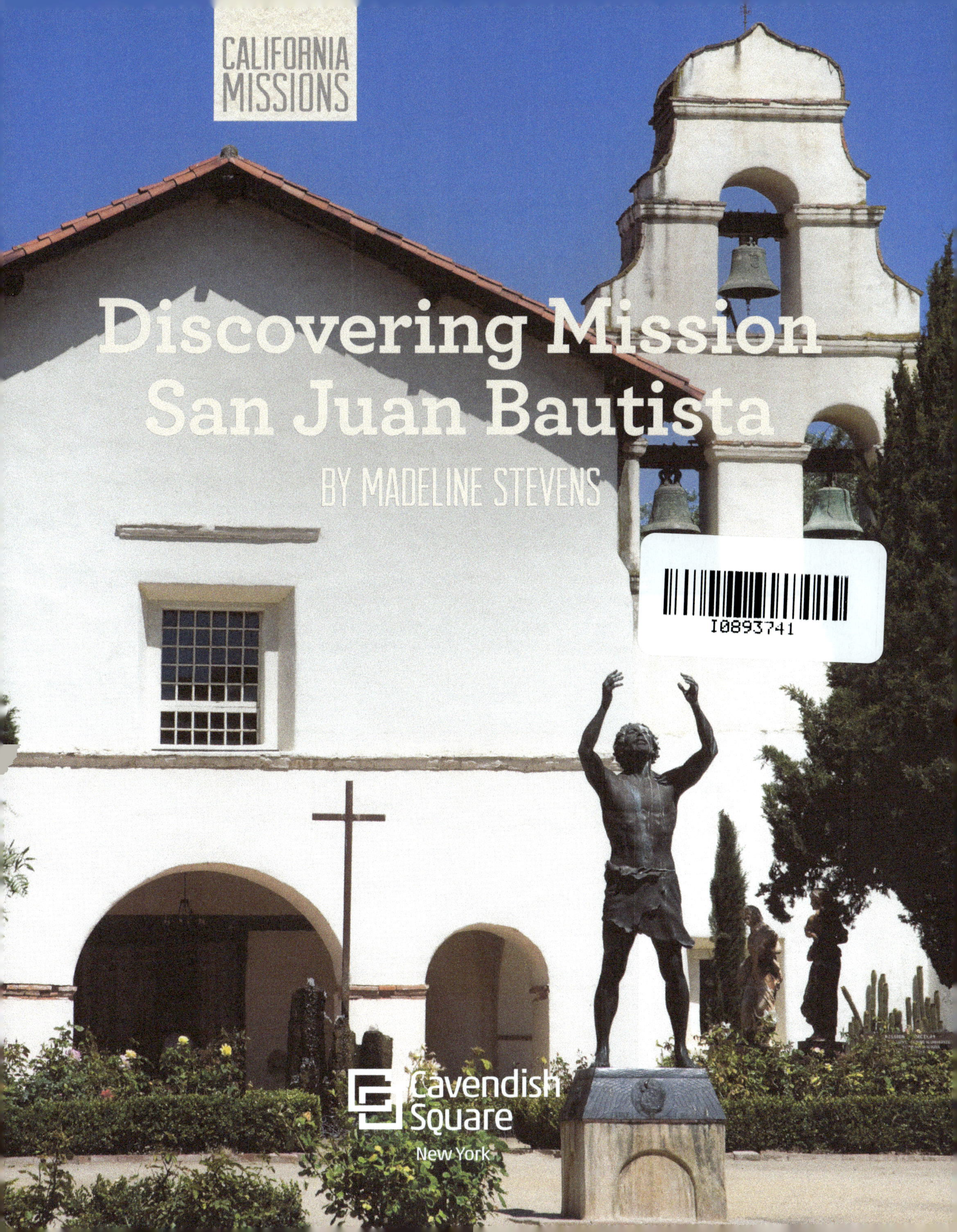

CALIFORNIA MISSIONS

Discovering Mission San Juan Bautista

BY MADELINE STEVENS

Cavendish Square
New York

Published in 2016 by Cavendish Square Publishing, LLC
243 5th Avenue, Suite 136, New York, NY 10016

First Edition

CPSIA Compliance Information: Batch #CW16CSQ

Library of Congress Cataloging-in-Publication Data

Stevens, Madeline.
Discovering Mission San Juan Bautista / Madeline Stevens.
pages cm. — (California missions)
Includes index.
ISBN 978-1-6271-3073-8 (hardcover) ISBN 978-1-5026-1213-7 (paperback) ISBN 978-1-6271-3075-2 (ebook)
1. San Juan Bautista (Mission : San Juan Bautista, Calif.)—History—Juvenile literature.
2. Spanish mission buildings—California—San Juan Bautista—History—Juvenile literature. 3. Franciscans—California—San Juan Bautista—History—Juvenile literature. 4. Ohlone Indians—Missions—California—San Juan Bautista—History—Juvenile literature. 5. Yokuts Indians—Missions—California—San Juan Bautista—History—Juvenile literature.
6. California—History—To 1846—Juvenile literature. I. Title.

F869.S3947S74 2015
979.4'75—dc23

2014005334

Editorial Director: Dean Miller
Editor: Kristen Susienka
Copy Editor: Cynthia Roby
Art Director: Jeffrey Talbot
Designer: Douglas Brooks
Photo Researcher: J8 Media
Production Manager: Jennifer Ryder-Talbot
Production Editor: David McNamara

The photographs in this book are used by permission and used through the courtesy of: Cover photo by Urban/File:Mission San Juan Bautista.jpg/Wikimedia Commons; Richard Cummins/Lonely Planet Images/Getty Images, 1; Witold Skrypczak/Lonely Planet Images/Getty Images, 4; North Wind/North Wind Picture Archives, 6; De Agostini/Getty Images, 8; Library of Congress Prints and Photographs Division, 10; Courtesy of UC Berkley/Bancroft Library, 12–13; © 2014 Pentacle Press, 15; Nicholas Pavloff/Lonely Planet Images/Getty Images, 17; National Archives and Records Administration/File:Making and curing adobe bricks - NARA - 286037.tif/Wikimedia Commons, 19; © 2012 Pentacle Press, 20; File:Sanjuanbautistamission.jpg/Wikimedia Commons, 23; Malgorzata Litkowska/Shutterstock.com, 26; Unknown/File:FlorentineCodex BK12 F54 smallpox.jpg/Wikimedia Commons, 29; © North Wind/North Wind Picture Archives, 31; Unknown/File:Manuel Micheltorena.jpg/Wikimedia Commons, 33; Zack Frank/Shutterstock.com, 34; Urban/File:Mission San Juan Bautista.jpg/Wikimedia Commons, 41.

Printed in the United States of America

CALIFORNIA MISSIONS

Contents

Mission San Juan Bautista has been restored to appear as it looked in the early 1800s.

1 The Spanish in the Americas

The rolling Gabilan Mountains in California shelter the beautiful city of San Juan Bautista. Many say that walking into San Juan Bautista is like stepping back in time. Quaint houses line dusty streets, bronze church bells sound through a blue sky. As home to one of the oldest missions in California, there is no doubting that San Juan Bautista has an olden-days feel.

The city of San Juan Bautista was named for a **mission** that was built there more than 215 years ago: Mission San Juan Bautista. Founded on June 24, 1797, it was the fifteenth of twenty-one missions built by the Spanish along the coast of present-day California, from San Diego to Sonoma.

THE SPANISH ARRIVE IN ALTA CALIFORNIA

Europeans had inhabited the New World (South America, Central America, and North America) since the late 1400s. But by the late 1700s, the Spanish had not explored the California region for nearly 200 years since the 1602 expedition of Sebastián Vizcaíno. Spain's new interest in this part of the world was sparked by a desire to expand its **empire** and to establish fortresses in the largely decolonized California region. At that time, what are now present-day California and the Baja Peninsula were known as *Alta* (meaning "higher") California and *Baja* (meaning "lower") California. Present-day Mexico was known as New Spain.

In the late 1700s, the Spanish government sent a group of **Franciscan** *frays* (Spanish word meaning **friars**) from New Spain to Alta California. The friars were tasked with establishing mission settlements that would be set up close to the soldiers' *presidios*, or fortresses. The Spanish wanted the priests to **convert** the Native California people living along the coast to **Christianity** and teach them how to become Spanish citizens. By claiming more land and the Native people living there, the Spanish hoped to ward off any other people from other countries that also wanted to live in California. This move would also offer the Spanish government a larger part of the world to control.

The Franciscans believed in living simply, studying the Bible, and teaching others about their religion. They were dedicated to their task and journeyed to the mission locations, and held good intentions for both their country and the people they would meet. Little did they realize that by teaching the Native Americans to be like the Spanish, they would destroy many tribal cultures and change the lives of those involved forever.

2
The Amah Mutsun People

The Native people encountered by the missionaries who started Mission San Juan Bautista were from the Amah Mutsun tribe, a branch of the Ohlone nation.

Although the exact date the Mutsun tribe arrived in the San Juan area is unknown, artifactual evidence estimates their presence there to have been as many as 3,000 years ago. Within a stretch of 40 to 50 miles (64 to 80 kilometers) were several Mutsun villages. They settled in a triangular region of land between the Monterey Bay and the Pajaro and San Benito rivers, an area rich in water and fish. Each of these tribes spoke slightly different dialects, or versions, of one language. They shared basic methods of hunting, fishing, cooking, and building. They also held the same traditions and religious beliefs, and were skilled craftsmen.

HOUSING AND CLOTHING

The Mutsuns lived in beehive-shaped huts that they wove from flexible branches, **tule** reeds, and willow leaves. These houses were perfectly suited to the mild weather in central California. It was warm during most of the year, and it rarely snowed. In the summer, it was so warm that the Mutsun women dressed in short aprons and the men often wore nothing at all. In the winter, both men and women wore cloaks of animal skin.

HUNTERS AND GATHERERS

Mutsun men fished and hunted for food. Using the resources around them, they made their own bows, arrows, and spears for hunting. Fishing was especially important to them, and salmon was a fish they ate often. They hunted squirrels, rabbits, otters, and larger game, such as elk and deer. One method to hunt deer

The Native people hunted on land and fished to catch good food to eat.

involved camouflage: the hunter disguised himself by wearing a deer head and fur.

The women gathered plants, acorns, berries, and seeds to eat. Acorns were a very important source of nutrition for the Mutsuns, and the women ground them into flour to make porridge and breads. Because acorns contain an acid, the women rinsed the flour with water ten times to make it safe for cooking. Then they let the flour dry and stored it for later use.

CRAFTS AND GAMES

The Mutsun women made baskets from grasses and strips of wood. The baskets were used to store food, carry supplies, hold water, trap fish, and cook. Other crafts the Mutsuns enjoyed making included jewelry and musical instruments. They carved flutes and whistles from the bones of geese and deer. They made rattles by filling hollow sticks, gourds, and cocoons with gravel. They also enjoyed singing and dancing.

RITUALS AND BELIEFS

The Mutsuns held many beliefs and rituals that were specific to their culture. They believed that all living things—plants, animals, and nature—had spirits and should be respected. It was even forbidden to hunt, kill, or eat specific animals.

Although the Amah Mutsuns hunted and killed animals for food the way the Europeans did, they had a respect for life that was sometimes hard for the Europeans to understand. For example, it was traditional for a Mutsun hunter or fisher to respond to a

Friars such as Junípero Serra, the first leader of the Alta California mission system, started missions to convert the Native people.

catch with a feeling of respect for the death of a fellow creature. In the same situation, a European hunter might be pleased rather than sad. When the Spanish began to convert the Mutsuns to Christianity, they not only changed the religious ideas of the Mutsuns, but also their way of looking at the world. As a result, many parts of Mutsun culture, not just the games and rituals but the different ways in which the Mutsuns understood the world, were forgotten or lost.

3 The Mission System

The mission system of Alta California consisted of twenty-one different religious communities set up along the coast of present-day California between 1769 and 1823. The concept of a mission had been introduced centuries earlier, with the arrival of the first Christians in other parts of the world. However, the mission system created by the Spanish would bring Christianity to the Native population of the largely unexplored West.

TROUBLE FROM ABROAD

In the 1700s, the Alta California region of the New World was a popular place for countries to expand their rule. Spain was not the only country that wanted part of California. The Russians and the British also sought after areas in northern California and set up forts. The race for land had begun.

In the 1760s, Spain's king Carlos III viewed Russia and other countries as major threats to Spain's claim on the land. His solution was to send Spanish priests from the Franciscan order of the **Catholic** Church to Alta California to start missions. Several missions were already running in both New Spain and Baja California, and seemed to do well. The hope was for the Spanish friars to work with the Native people, teaching them how to live as Spaniards, speak their language, and worship their Christian god. By having control of the land and the people of this region, Spain would also expand its rule and overpower any country that stood in its way.

The idea behind the missions was that the friars would travel to an area to meet, and then convert, the Native residents. The converted Native people would then live and work at the mission. After the missions were established and running well, the mission and its lands would be handed back to the Native people to manage it. The Native people would learn and accept Spanish customs, and be considered Spanish citizens. This would allow for Spain's continuing rule over the land and the people.

Mission San Juan Bautista was one of twenty-one missions in Alta California.

THE FIRST MISSION

To bring the Alta California mission system into existence, land close to a Native village boasting good soil for farming and a reliable source of water was necessary. The effort also required the leadership of a friar. The first mission, San Diego de Alcalá, had all of these things. It was started in 1769 and led by Fray Junípero Serra, who would become the founder and president of the first nine missions in Alta California.

After the first mission was established, others soon followed. Each new mission signaled a new part of Alta California for the Spanish empire. However, through these successes, damage was done to the Native people who both lived in the area and were brought to live and work at the mission.

4 The Birth of the Mission

Mission San Juan Bautista was built to bridge the gap between missions San Carlos Borroméo del Río Carmelo and Santa Cruz along the road El Camino Real. El Camino Real served as an easy way to travel along the coast and connected all the Alta California missions. The road was designed so that each mission was only one day's ride from the other. The Franciscans and the Spanish government wanted the missions to make travel along the coast of Alta California easy. The Spanish did not feel safe traveling through the lands of the Native people because they feared being attacked or even killed. Mission San Juan Bautista shortened the stretch between missions San Carlos Borroméo del Río Carmelo and Santa Cruz that left travelers vulnerable to confrontations on the open road.

Teaching Christianity to the First Californians was not the missions' only purpose. They also offered shelter and safety to traveling Spanish settlers who wanted to settle in Alta California. The government of New Spain knew that the sooner Alta California was populated with Spanish citizens, the sooner it would really belong to Spain. Therefore, it was important to make the area as safe and welcoming to Spanish settlers as possible.

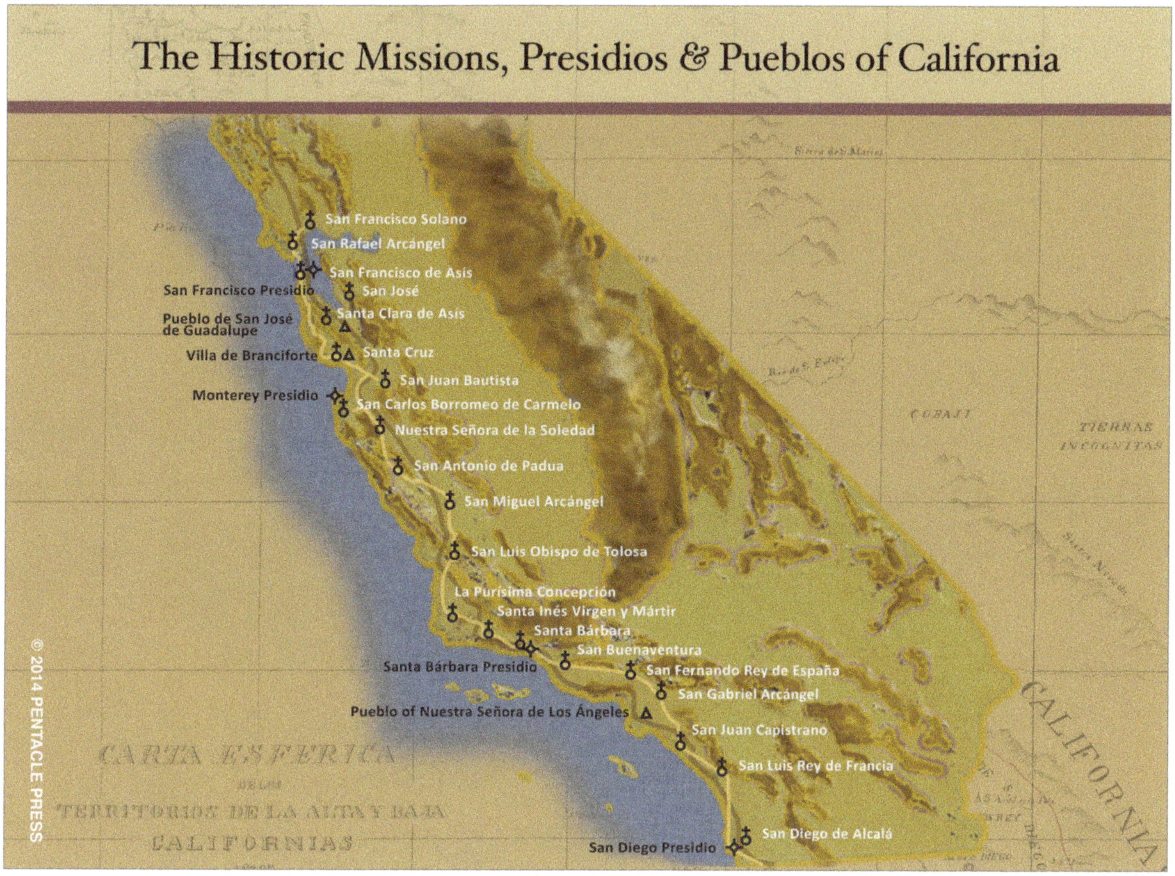

Each mission was connected by a road called El Camino Real (illustrated by the yellow line), parts of which are still visible today.

A SITE IS FOUND

In the late 1700s, the head of the mission system, Fray Fermín Francisco de Lasuén, wanted to establish new missions in the areas near the populations of Native Californians. The founders of Mission San Juan Bautista traveled in 1795 to an area of land close to the village of Popeloutchom, where the Amah Mutsun tribe lived.

A soldier named Hermenegildo Sal led the expedition to locate the perfect mission site. Fray Antonio Dantí, who kept a record of the trip, accompanied him. The party set out on November 15, 1795.

Along the journey, Fray Dantí wrote that they saw "few Native people, as well as an abandoned native village consisting of twenty-seven homes." The small number of indigenous Californians in the area worried the friars. They wanted to find a large population of people to convert and use to work on the mission. If there were too few Native people, there would be no one to convert, and farming and building at the mission would not be successful.

The expedition party reached the banks of the San Benito River on November 16, 1795. On the 17th, they examined the plain below the river and found two pools that could be used as wells. They also located willow, poplar, alder, and redwood trees for timber, tule for roofing, and limestone for building foundations. The soil was excellent for farming and gardening. Sal and Dantí decided that the area looked like a good place for a mission. They set up a large cross to mark the spot. The cross symbolized the Christian religion and showed that they were claiming the area for the Spanish government.

When Fray Lasuén received Dantí's report, he thought the site was ideal. It was well placed to close the distance between missions San Carlos Borroméo del Río Carmelo and Santa Cruz. Near the site and west toward the coast stood many Mutsun villages. And in the valley to the south: Yokut tribes.

FOUNDING CELEBRATIONS

Almost two years later, on June 24, 1797, Mission San Juan Bautista was founded. Fray Lasuén traveled to perform the founding ceremony himself. He blessed the site, performed a

Mass, and named frays José Manuel de Martiarena and Pedro Adriano Martinez as the first friars of the mission.

The size of the cross placed at Mission San Juan Bautista impressed the Mutsun and Yokut people. A legend spread among these tribes that the cross was more powerful than the local Native altars. The Mutsun and Yokut began to believe that the Spaniards were powerful shamans, or magic users. Many Mutsuns and Yokuts began to believe that it was wise to stand in the shadow of the cross and become Christians. Perhaps even more convincing than the cross were the gifts that the Spanish gave them. The Mutsuns and Yokuts who attended the founding ceremony were given food, as well as beads and other trinkets. They were encouraged to stay and work.

Many Native people thought the cross that the friars and soldiers set up at the grounds of Mission San Juan Bautista was powerful, and because of this, many people converted.

5 The Early Days of the Mission

Soon after the founding ceremony, work on the mission began. Temporary buildings were quickly constructed out of wooden planks and then covered with mud roofs. Stormy weather and earthquakes could damage these buildings easily. They could also catch fire from open flames when cooking food or heating the buildings.

The friars eventually wanted their mission to be made of more secure materials. Like most of the missions in Alta California, Mission San Juan Bautista would be constructed of **adobe** bricks coated with white plaster. Adobe is a mixture of soil, water, and cut straw that is hardened in the sunlight, and buildings made from this material stay cool in the summer and warm in the winter.

Fray Martiarena and Fray Martinez worked quickly to begin construction on the adobe buildings at the mission. They enlisted the help of soldiers and members of the Mutsun and Yokut tribes, who were curious about the arrival of the Spanish and the many interesting objects, jewelry, and weapons they had. Many Native people joined the mission as **neophytes**, or newly converted Christians.

BUILDING IMPROVES

The builders at Mission San Juan Bautista worked quickly. By December 31, 1797, construction on nine buildings had been completed. An adobe chapel, measuring 42 x 17 feet (12.8 x 5.2 meters), was built and roofed with mud and tule. A home for the missionaries was made of the same materials. Also constructed was a **granary** for grain storage; a *monjerío*, or house for unmarried women; a kitchen, and a guardhouse. Housing for the soldiers at the mission was also built. In 1803, work on the present-day church began and it was officially finished in 1812. Other buildings followed and were completed between 1800 and 1812.

The church at Mission San Juan Bautista was the largest and most unusual of the mission churches. Most of the others were

People at the mission made adobe bricks by hand and laid them side-by-side to dry in the sun.

Mission friars baptized many people, both young and old, into the Christian religion, usually by pouring water over them.

long and narrow and had only one section of seats. Mission San Juan Bautista's church had three sections of seats that were able to accommodate about a thousand people.

The friars were building San Juan Bautista much like the other missions: in the shape of a quadrangle, or open square. The mission quadrangle would include the church, the friars' living quarters, the monjerío, kitchens, dining rooms, workshops, storage rooms, and granaries. The mission's open square held a courtyard. Outside its walls was the *ranchería,* or the neophyte village, orchards, fields, corrals for the animals, and the cemetery. *Ranchos* were established a few miles (kilometers) away from the mission, where there was more land for grazing the **livestock**. Each rancho usually had a house for the neophytes, a chapel, and a corral.

The work of **ranching** began right away. It was important to have animals to take care of and to provide as food for the people at the mission. Initially, livestock for Mission San Juan Bautista was donated from other missions. In its first year, the mission had 115 cattle, 140 sheep, 4 pigs, and 6 horses. Farming, another important part of the mission system, did not begin until the following year.

THE PEOPLE OF THE MISSION

As the building and ranching progressed, frays Martiarena and Martinez were also teaching the Mutsuns and Yokuts. They schooled those who were curious about the Christian religion, and taught them to speak the Spanish language. When the friars felt that the Native people had learned enough about Christianity, they **baptized** them and welcomed them to the mission as neophytes.

The neophytes had to live at the mission and obey the friars, adjusting from life in a tribe to life in a religious community. As a result, they could not visit their old villages, practice their old religion, or live as they had before they were baptized. The friars and soldiers controlled every part of the neophytes' lives from the moment they arrived at the mission. If they disobeyed, they could be punished, which often meant being beaten.

At first, some neophytes entered the mission willingly. They believed in the power of the Christian god and were interested in the different objects the Spanish brought with them, such as colored beads, guns, and horses. However, after a time, they became unhappy with the life there. Some even escaped and returned to their old villages. Friars then had to send soldiers into the villages to bring the escaped neophytes back to the mission.

FAULT OF THE FRIARS

What Fray Dantí and Hermenegildo Sal did not know when they recommended the site for Mission San Juan Bautista was that the land they chose lay on a fault, or a split beneath Earth's surface that causes earthquakes. The mission had been built directly on the San Andreas fault, and thereby suffered many earthquakes during its lifetime.

October 1800 was a particularly bad month at Mission San Juan Bautista. Those living at the mission reported six earthquakes a day for nineteen days. All of the mission buildings were badly damaged and had to be reconstructed.

A COMMUNITY GROWS

At the end of 1800, Mission San Juan Bautista had grown into a community. More than 500 neophytes had converted and come to live at the mission. Together they had harvested 2,700 bushels of grain that year, and the number of livestock was steadily increasing. The mission was quickly becoming a self-sustaining place that could grow, raise, or make almost everything it needed.

6
Mission Life

Day-to-day, Mission San Juan Bautista followed a strict agenda. Bells rang to call the neophytes to wake, pray, eat, and work. This way of life was not always an easy adjustment for those men, women, and children involved.

BELLS OF THE MISSION

The bells were important parts of the mission system. They let people know when to move on to their next activity. The morning bell would ring around 6 a.m., alerting everyone that it was time to wake. Everyone would then gather in the church to celebrate Mass, a Catholic ceremony that praises and celebrates God. After the service they would eat breakfast, which usually consisted of *atole*, a type of porridge made from corn. Once breakfast was finished, everyone would go off to work. At noon,

The bells at Mission San Juan Bautista rang to signal new activities.

the bells would ring for lunch, which usually was *pozole*, another soup with beans and peas. Once lunch had been eaten, they had a few hours to relax. This was called a *siesta*. After that, more work would be done. When the final bell rang, all work was to stop.

CHORES AT THE MISSION

Men, women, and children were tasked with a variety of chores around the mission. Women would spend time making clothes, dishes, and shoes, carding wool and cotton, sewing shirts and dresses, knitting socks, and weaving blankets. They also swept and mopped both the mission buildings and the church, and washed clothes in the *lavandería*, or washing area. Unmarried girls and women worked in the kitchens, the kitchen garden, or the sewing room. They made bread, prepared stews, and ground olives into oil. Sometimes they would also tend to the gardens and orchards, and help out on the farms. In the orchards, they tended the grapevines and the fig, pear, and olive trees that the friars had imported from Spain. Men would also help in the gardens, and spent most of their days building, farming, or tending to livestock. Children attended religious classes taught by the friars, and worked in the orchard gathering fruit and watching the animals.

RELAXATION AND SLEEP

The neophytes usually relaxed following dinner. It was during this time that they could participate in some pastime activities, such as building crafts, playing games, or singing and dancing. They were usually required to pray before going to bed. All neophytes had to be in bed by 8 or 9 p.m., though the women often had an earlier curfew than the men.

LIVING AT MISSION SAN JUAN BAUTISTA

When the mission began, it was difficult for the friars and the neophytes to communicate. Neither party spoke the other's language, and the strict daily schedule often made the Native people unhappy. Because the friars believed that unmarried women should live apart from men, families were separated. Unmarried women and girls over the age of 11 had to live in the monjerío. When a girl reached 15 or 16, she moved from the monjerío to other female dormitories, hoping to meet and marry a young man. After she had married, she and her husband could then move into a house in the ranchería and raise a family.

CROPS AND ANIMALS

At Mission San Juan Bautista, many crops grew and many animals roamed. The main crops were barley, wheat, corn, beans, and peas. Olives, however, were the most important crop because from them, olive oil was produced. Olive oil was important to the mission's survival as it was used in the trading between settlers, Natives, and other missions for supplies. Animals also helped the mission survive. Sheep and cattle made up the majority of the mission's livestock, but there were also pigs, horses, and mules. Cattle were especially important because such livestock served as one of the mission's greatest resources for food. Records show that fifty cows were killed every week to feed the mission community.

THE IMPORTANCE OF OLIVES

One of the most important jobs at Mission San Juan Bautista was making olive oil. Neophytes gathered olives from the orchard. Then they poured them into a stone olive mill. Next a mule was tied to a wooden beam attached to the mill and was led in a circle. This movement turned a giant stone at the bottom of the mill and crushed the olives. The women then pressed the oil from the crushed olives and stored it in large clay jars.

Olives were very important to the mission because they allowed the mission to make and sell olive oil.

In the early days, the neophytes either grew or created almost everything that was needed at the mission. As time went on, and more and more people settled in Alta California, the friars were able to trade for items that the mission's neophytes could not make. Through trade, they received tools and supplies such as iron kettles and pottery, and some luxury items including silk, coffee, honey, and decorations for the mission church.

7 Hardship and Decline

As the years passed, life at Mission San Juan Bautista became difficult for the neophytes. This led not only to hardship but also to a decrease in population.

ATTEMPTS TO ESCAPE

From the beginning, neophytes struggled to adjust to life at the mission. They missed their old ways of life and their tribes. The strict schedule set by the friars left little time for the Native people to participate in activities they once enjoyed. Also, the friars required that any traces of Native life be eliminated from the mission. This included language and religious practices. Being forced to surrender their culture led many neophytes to practice their language and beliefs in secret. It also encouraged many to escape.

In 1805, it was recorded that 200 neophytes had run away from Mission San Juan Bautista. Although this was quite a large number, more Native Californians remained in the mission because the friars had been actively converting people in the area. Because the neophytes did most of the work that made the mission productive, the missionaries were always interested in increasing the neophyte population.

Despite their good intentions, the friars did not understand that the neophytes deserved to live the way they always had or that their culture was just as important and valuable as their own. This led to uncomfortable, and sometimes terrible, situations. For example, in an effort to recruit more neophytes for the mission, friars would sometimes send soldiers into the villages. The soldiers did not always treat the Native people with respect. Some Native people were converted by the soldiers and brought to the mission against their will.

In 1806, Spanish army officer Gabriel Moraga, accompanied by soldiers and friars, led an expedition to establish other missions farther inland. The group managed to convert 141 indigenous people—all were quite old or dying. It was often easier for the friars to convert people who were sick or about to die. Believing that only baptized Christians would go to heaven, the friars frightened these people by describing to them all the terrible things that would happen after their death. Only then did many of them agree to be baptized.

A BRIEF TIME OF HAPPINESS

In 1812, the friars of Mission San Juan Bautista were honored by mission president Fray Estévan Tapis, as he made the decision to retire there. Fray Tapis had a passion for music and created a choir of young neophyte boys. He invented a special way of color-coding the music so that the boys could read it and follow along as Fray Tapis played the pipe organ. Tapis ran the choir with the help of Fray Felipe de la Cuesta. Fray Cuesta took interest in the culture of the neophytes at the mission, later recording the vocabulary and grammar of the Mutsun language. Fray Cuesta became the most prolific chronicler of the indigenous languages of Alta California during the mission period.

DISEASE AND DEATH

The biggest problem at Mission San Juan Bautista, and at every other Alta California mission, was the threat of disease for the indigenous people. When the Spanish arrived from Europe, they brought with them illnesses such as measles and smallpox.

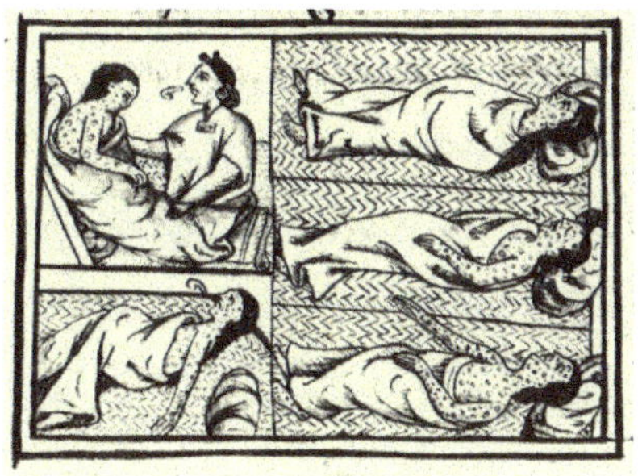

Diseases hurt or killed many people at the missions.

Because the indigenous people had never been exposed to these diseases, their immune systems were not strong enough to fight them off. Many Native people, both at the mission and in the surrounding villages, died as a result. There were also reports of entire villages of people dying.

ATTACKS AND ABANDONMENT

Throughout its early years, Mission San Juan Bautista was attacked often by the tribes living in the area near to the mission. In 1815 and 1816, bands of the Yokut tribe stormed the mission several times, stealing horses and murdering some of the neophytes. Between 1818 and 1819, seventy-nine neophytes ran away from the mission. In late 1819, a group of Yokuts raided the mission and stole nearly forty mares and mules. The noise of the attack woke a group of neophytes, who chased the thieves and recaptured the animals.

ACTS OF NATURE

As you have read, earthquakes played a role in devastating Mission San Juan Bautista. Throughout the 1800s and into the 1900s, the mission's church and other buildings required repairs on numerous occasions because of the damaging effects earthquakes had on the mission. The worst earthquakes were the ones that happened at Santa Barbara in October of 1800, and the Great San Francisco Earthquake of 1906.

CHANGES

The year 1821 brought significant changes to the missions. New Spain and Spain had been at war since 1810, and in 1821 New Spain—renamed Mexico—won its independence. This meant Mexico now had control over the Alta California area and all of the missions established there. Despite this, the mission system continued to grow. In 1823, the neophyte population at Mission San Juan Bautista was 1,248. This was the largest number of neophytes that would ever be at the mission. During this year, the last of the missions, Mission San Francisco Solano, was also started.

The new government, however, decided in the 1830s to secularize the missions. This would change the missions and the lives of all involved.

8
Secularization

In 1833, the Mexican government passed a law called the Act of **Secularization**. Secularization meant taking financial control of the missions away from the Catholic Church and the Franciscans. Many of the Catholic priests were removed from the missions and sent back to Spain. Replacing them were Mexican priests

During secularization many Native people left the missions to start new lives as ranch hands for landowners elsewhere.

who had different ways of managing the missions. The Mexican government sold most of the land to wealthy ranchers. Mexican officials were sent to run the mission lands that were not sold and to rule over those neophytes who did not leave the missions. The missions would no longer be used to convert indigenous Californians to Christianity.

SECULARIZATION AT MISSION SAN JUAN BAUTISTA

Mission San Juan Bautista was officially secularized in 1835. Neophytes had mixed feelings, however. Many were fearful at the thought of leaving because they were born at the mission and knew nothing of life outside of it. Others embraced their freedom and traveled to the growing cities of California to look for work. Some returned to their tribes.

The Mexican government attempted to provide for these Native people by giving them some of the mission lands and livestock. Half of the mission lands were made into a group farm called a *pueblo de indios*, or "Indian town," which was managed by the mission's ex-neophytes. This arrangement did not work well. After years of taking orders from the friars, the neophytes found it difficult to run the mission without a leader. They also had to deal with ranchers who wanted to take the mission lands for themselves. Constant Yokut raids interfered with any attempts to continue farming. By 1840, even the orchards of Mission San Juan Bautista were nearly ruined. All the neophytes had abandoned the area and only fifty Californians who lived around the San Juan Bautista church remained.

THE END OF THE MISSIONS: GOVERNOR MICHELTORENA

The last hero of the Alta California mission system was Governor Manuel Micheltorena, who, in the 1840s, briefly returned the missions to the Franciscans. He was ultimately unsuccessful, however, and the missions returned to the Mexican authorities.

SELLING THE MISSION

Governor Micheltorena was replaced in February 1845 by Governor Pio de Jesús Pico, who viewed the rich farmland of the failing mission system as a chance to make money. On September 4, 1845, Governor Pico took an inventory of the goods and crops at Mission San Juan Bautista. He estimated the total value of the mission to be 7,860 *pesos*, the Mexican unit of money—or $591.08 in U.S. dollars. Pico then sold it in a secret auction. It was not until 1859 that President James Buchanan ordered that San Juan Bautista, along with 55 acres (22.3 hectares) of land, go back to the Catholic Church.

In the 1840s, Governor Manuel Micheltorena tried to return the missions to the Franciscans but was unsuccessful.

Today Mission San Juan Bautista flourishes as a tourist attraction and museum that preserves California's early history.

9
The Mission Alive Today

Mission San Juan Bautista remains today one of the most well-preserved Alta California missions. Its church has stood since 1812, and a priest has always been on the site—even through the years of secularization.

PRESERVATION EFFORTS

The church at Mission San Juan Bautista is the largest of all the mission churches. It looks almost exactly as it did nearly 211 years ago when the Mutsun and Yokut began its construction (1803).

The mission did suffer a violent earthquake in April 1906, during which the side walls of the church crumbled. But in 1907, the town held a *fiesta*, or festival, to raise money to restore the building. The repairs were eventually completed in 1976.

UNEARTHING HISTORY

Even though the main buildings of the mission are relatively unchanged, there is always more to learn about Mission San Juan Bautista. In 1991, an **archaeologist** named Glenn Farris explored the soil underneath the old ranchería. There he discovered two buildings buried under years of debris.

The buildings, both over 200 feet (61 m) long, were probably the homes of neophyte families. The smaller building has eleven rooms, the larger one, twenty-two rooms. Inside the buildings Farris found artifacts representing daily life: pestles for grinding acorns into flour, iron scissors and a brass thimble for sewing clothes, knives from New Spain, and jewelry made from shells and glass trade beads. A 10-inch (25.4-cm) **ramrod** for packing gunpowder into a pistol was also uncovered.

PRESERVING THE MUTSUN TRIBE

While Mission San Juan Bautista did colonize California for Spain and brought many new traditions and experiences, the missions greatly affected the lives of the indigenous people who lived there. Many aspects of their culture were lost: language, traditions, and heritage. For some time, efforts have been made for the government to recognize the Amah Mutsun as a true Native nation.

VISITING THE MISSION

Today Mission San Juan Bautista offers tourists many opportunities to view its grounds and discover the artifacts around it. Tourists can enter the church and observe the paintings and other small features that make it unique, stroll along the grounds observing the wildlife, or walk into the mission courtyard. There they can view the unchanged range of the Gabilan Mountains and appreciate the beauty surrounding them.

10
Make Your Own Mission Model

To make your own model of the San Juan Bautista mission, you will need:

- ruler
- Foam Core board
- scissors
- X-ACTO® knife (Ask for an adult's help)
- beige paint
- cardboard
- masking tape
- glue
- toothpicks
- white paint
- sand
- miniature bells
- artificial flowers/trees

DIRECTIONS

Adult supervision is suggested.

Step 1: To make the base, cut a Foam Core board to measure 16"× 15" (40.6 × 38.1 centimeters). Paint this beige. Allow it to dry.

Step 2: For the façade (front) of the church, cut a piece of cardboard with dimensions as shown.

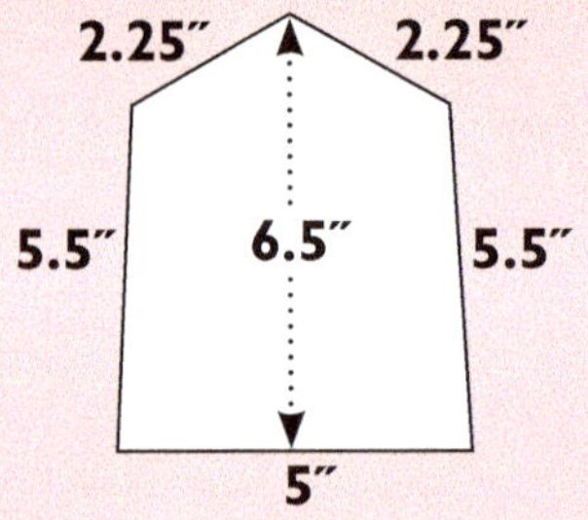

Step 3: Draw, and then cut out, doors and a window. Cut two pieces of cardboard measuring 1"× 5.5" (2.5 × 14 cm). Tape these to the sides of the façade as shown below.

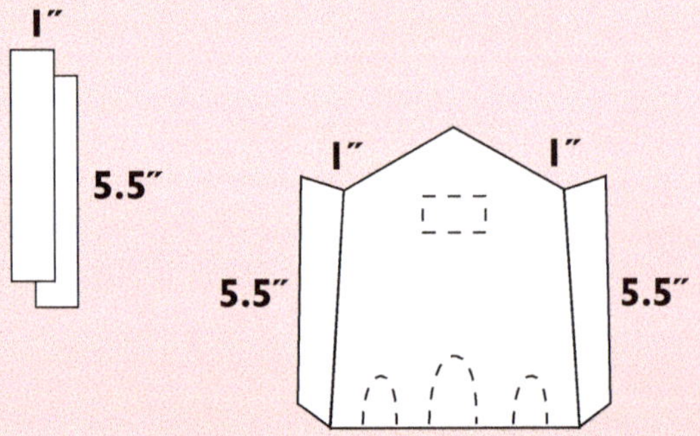

Step 4: For the sides of the church, cut two pieces of cardboard to measure 10"× 6" (25.4 × 15.2 cm). For the front and back, cut two pieces of cardboard to measure 6"× 6" (15.2 × 15.2 cm).

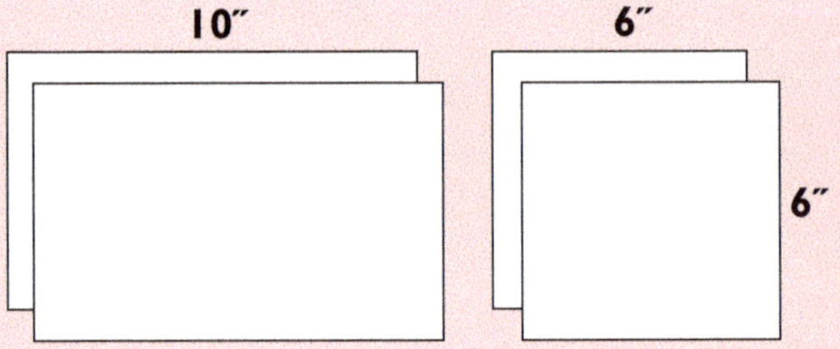

Step 5: Tape these pieces together to form a box shape. Then glue it to your base.

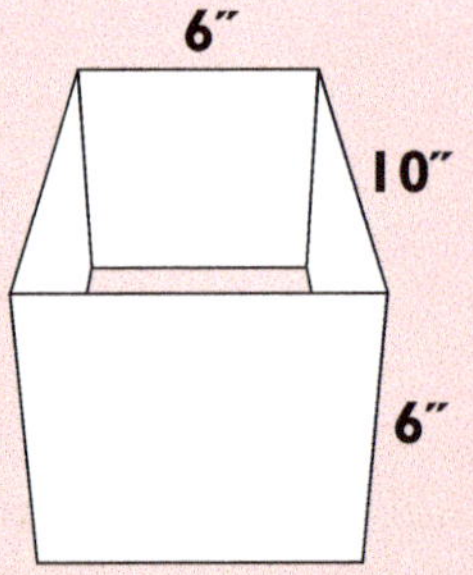

Step 6: Glue toothpicks horizontally and vertically to the inside of the façade window. Then tape the small sidewalls of the façade to the front of the box.

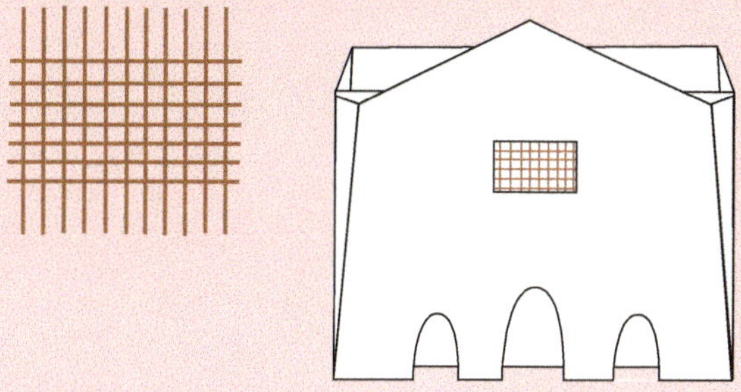

Step 7: To make the four building extensions on each corner of the church, cut 12 pieces of cardboard to measure 6" × 2" (15.2 × 5.1 cm).

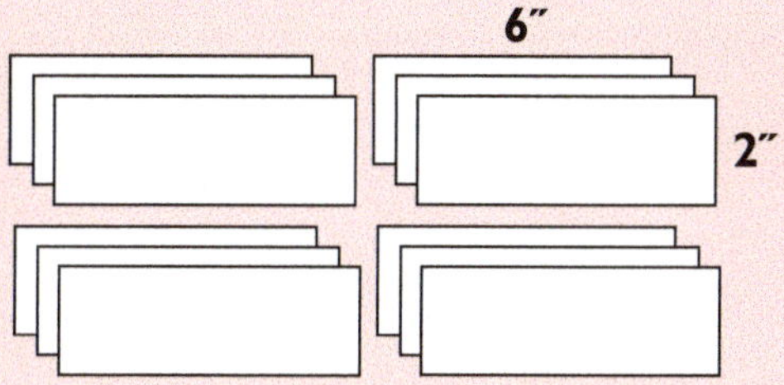

Step 8: Tape three of the pieces cut in Step 7 together to form a box shape with a missing side. Tape this to the left back corner of the church (the open end facing the church wall).

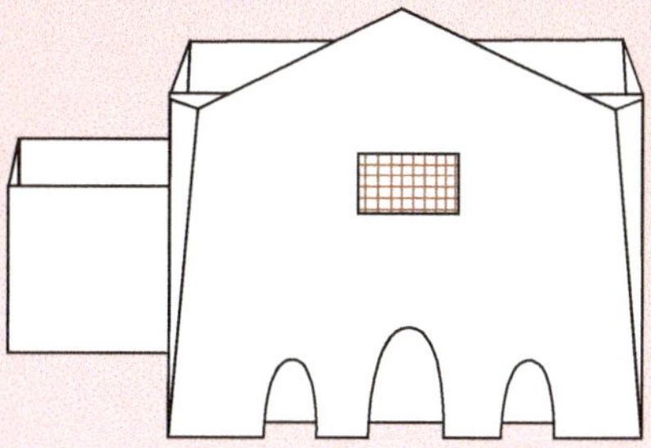

Step 9: Repeat this process three more times. Tape each three-sided structure to a corner of the church. Then glue them to the base.

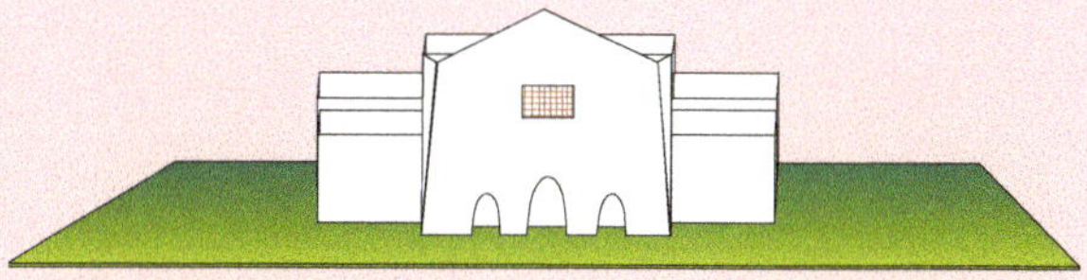

Step 10: For the bell tower, cut four pieces of cardboard to measure 2"× 3" (5.1 × 7.6 cm). Cut two large, arched windows out of one piece. This is where the two bells will hang.

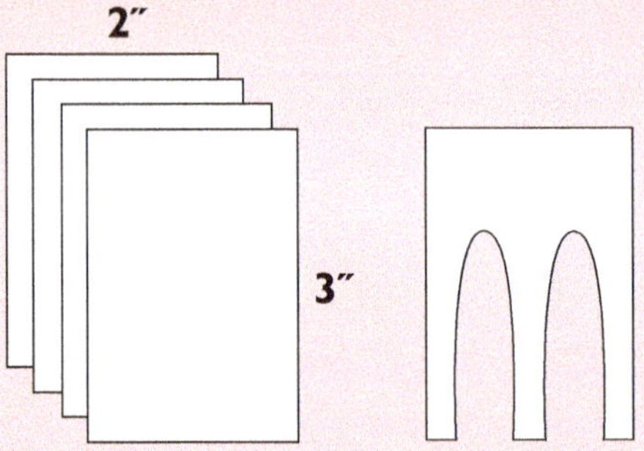

Step 11: Tape these four pieces together to form a box. Then tape this structure to the right front corner of the church.

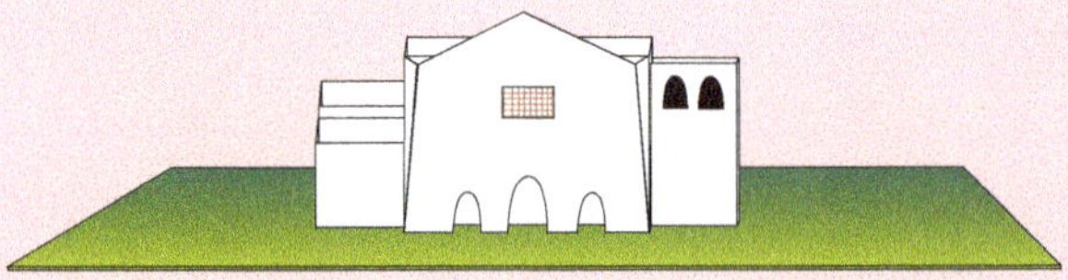

Step 12: Cut a piece of cardboard in the shape of an arch measuring 2"× 3" (5.1 × 7.6 cm). Cut out an arched window and tape this structure to the top of the bell tower.

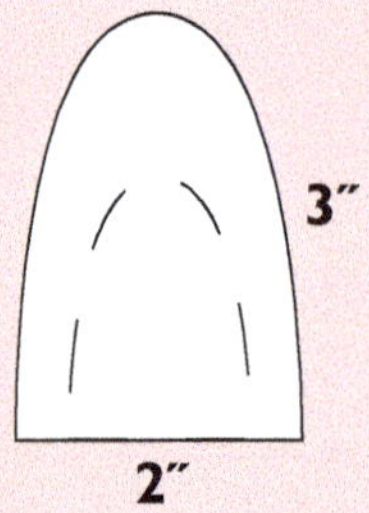

Step 13: Paint mission with white paint mixed with sand.

Step 14: For the roof, cut a piece of corrugated cardboard as shown here and glue to the top of the church.

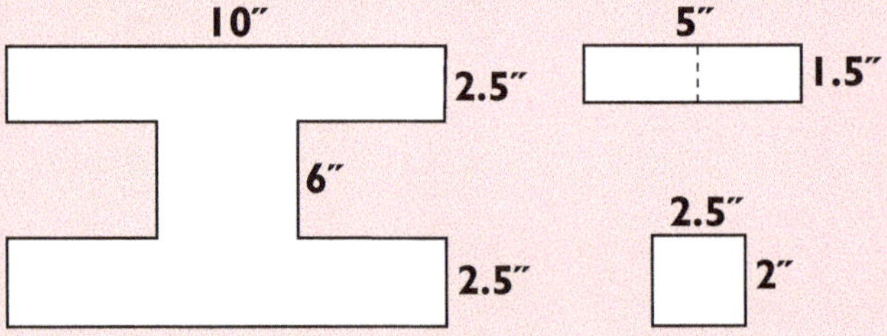

Step 15: Stick toothpicks through the bells, and glue them behind the windows. Decorate with greenery.

A completed model of Mission San Juan Bautista.

Key Dates in Mission History

1492	Christopher Columbus reaches the West Indies
1542	Cabrillo's expedition to California
1602	Sebastián Vizcaíno sails to California
1713	Fray Junípero Serra is born
1769	Founding of San Diego de Alcalá
1770	Founding of San Carlos Borroméo del Río Carmelo
1771	Founding of San Antonio de Padua and San Gabriel Arcángel
1772	Founding of San Luis Obispo de Tolosa
1775–76	Founding of San Juan Capistrano
1776	Founding of San Francisco de Asís
1776	Declaration of Independence is signed

1777	Founding of Santa Clara de Asís
1782	Founding of San Buenaventura
1784	Fray Serra dies
1786	Founding of Santa Bárbara
1787	Founding of La Purísima Concepción
1791	Founding of Santa Cruz and Nuestra Señora de la Soledad
1797	Founding of San José, San Juan Bautista, San Miguel Arcángel, and San Fernando Rey de España
1798	Founding of San Luis Rey de Francia
1804	Founding of Santa Inés
1817	Founding of San Rafael Arcángel
1823	Founding of San Francisco Solano
1833	Mexico passes Secularization Act
1848	Gold found in northern California
1850	California becomes the thirty-first state

Glossary

adobe (uh-DOH-bee) Sun-dried bricks made from straw, mud, and sometimes manure.

archaeologist (ar-kee-AH-luh-jist) A scientist who studies the bones, objects, buildings, and other remains of people from the past.

baptize (BAP-tyz) An act or ceremony performed when someone is accepted into, or accepts, the Christian faith.

Catholic (KATH-lik) A branch of Christianity which includes following the spiritual leadership of priests, who are headed by the Pope.

Christianity (kris-chee-AH-nih-tee) A religion based on the belief in Jesus Christ and the Bible; practiced by Eastern, Roman Catholic, and Protestant groups.

convert (kun-VIRT) To change from belief in one religion to belief in another religion.

empire (EM-pyr) A large area, usually including many different peoples, ruled by one government or leader.

Franciscan (fran-SIS-kin) A communal Roman Catholic order of friars, or "brothers," who follow the teachings and example of Saint Francis of Assisi, who did much work as a missionary.

friar (FRY-ur) A brother in a communal religious order. A friar can also be a priest.

granary (GRAY-nuh-ree) A building where grain is stored.

livestock (LYV-stahk) Farm animals kept for use or profit.

mission (MIH-shun) A religious community set up and run by members of the religious faith.

neophyte (NEE-oh-fyt) The term that describes someone who is newly converted to Christianity.

ramrod (RAM-rod) A metal stick used for packing gunpowder into a gun.

ranching (RAN-ching) Raising cattle, horses, or sheep on a farm.

secularization (seh-kyuh-luh-rih-ZAY-shun) When control of the missions' land was taken from the church and given to the government.

tule (TOO-lee) Reeds used by Native people to make houses and boats.

Pronunciation Guide

convento (kon-BEN-toh)

El Camino Real (EL kah-MEE-noh RAY-al)

fiesta (fee-EHS-tah)

fray (FRAY)

lavandería (lah-ban-deh-REE-ah)

monjerío (mohn-hay-REE-oh)

pueblo de indios (PWAY-blo de IN-dee-ohs)

ranchería (rahn-cheh-REE-ah)

rancho (RAHN-choh)

Find Out More

Check out these books and websites to learn more about Mission San Juan Bautista and the missions of California.

BOOKS

Abbink, Emily. *Monterey Bay Area Missions*. Minneapolis, MN: Lerner Publishing Group, 2008.

Bellezza, Robert A. *Images of America: Missions of Monterey*. Charleston, SC: Arcadia Publishing, 2012.

Gendell, Megan. *The Spanish Missions of California*. New York, NY: Scholastic, 2010.

Gibson, Karen Bush. *Native American History for Kids*. Chicago, IL: Chicago Review Press, 2010.

WEBSITES

Amah Mutsun Tribal Band of Ohlone/Costanoan People
www.icimedia.com/costanoan
Explore the history of the Amah Mutsun Tribal Band of Ohlone/Costanoan people.

California Missions Resource Center
www.missionscalifornia.com
Interact with a mission timeline, videos, and photo gallery and unlock key facts about each mission in the California mission system.

City of San Juan Bautista, California
www.san-juan-bautista.ca.us
Explore the city of San Juan Bautista today; view photos and learn about the city's events.

Old Mission San Juan Bautista
www.oldmissionsjb.org
Learn more about the old Mission San Juan Bautista.

Index

Page numbers in **boldface** are illustrations.